Rats

by Grace Hansen

Abdo
ANIMAL FRIENDS
Kids

abdopublishing.com

Published by Abdo Kids, a division of ABDO, PO Box 398166, Minneapolis, Minnesota 55439.

Copyright © 2016 by Abdo Consulting Group, Inc. International copyrights reserved in all countries. No part of this book may be reproduced in any form without written permission from the publisher.

Printed in the United States of America, North Mankato, Minnesota.

052015

092015

THIS BOOK CONTAINS
RECYCLED MATERIALS

Photo Credits: Glow Images, iStock, Shutterstock

Production Contributors: Teddy Borth, Jennie Forsberg, Grace Hansen

Design Contributors: Laura Rask, Dorothy Toth

Library of Congress Control Number: 2014958404

Cataloging-in-Publication Data

Hansen, Grace.

Rats / Grace Hansen.

p. cm. -- (Animal friends)

ISBN 978-1-62970-896-6

Includes index.

1. Rats--Juvenile literature.   I. Title.

599.35--dc23

2014958404

Table of Contents

Rats

Rats are **rodents**. Rats can be different colors. They can have **markings**, too.

Rats have hair. They have four

legs. They have pink noses.

Rats have long tails. They use their tails to **balance**.

8

Learning About Rats

Rats are often used in **experiments**. Scientists use rats to learn more about humans. They learn things about rats, too.

10

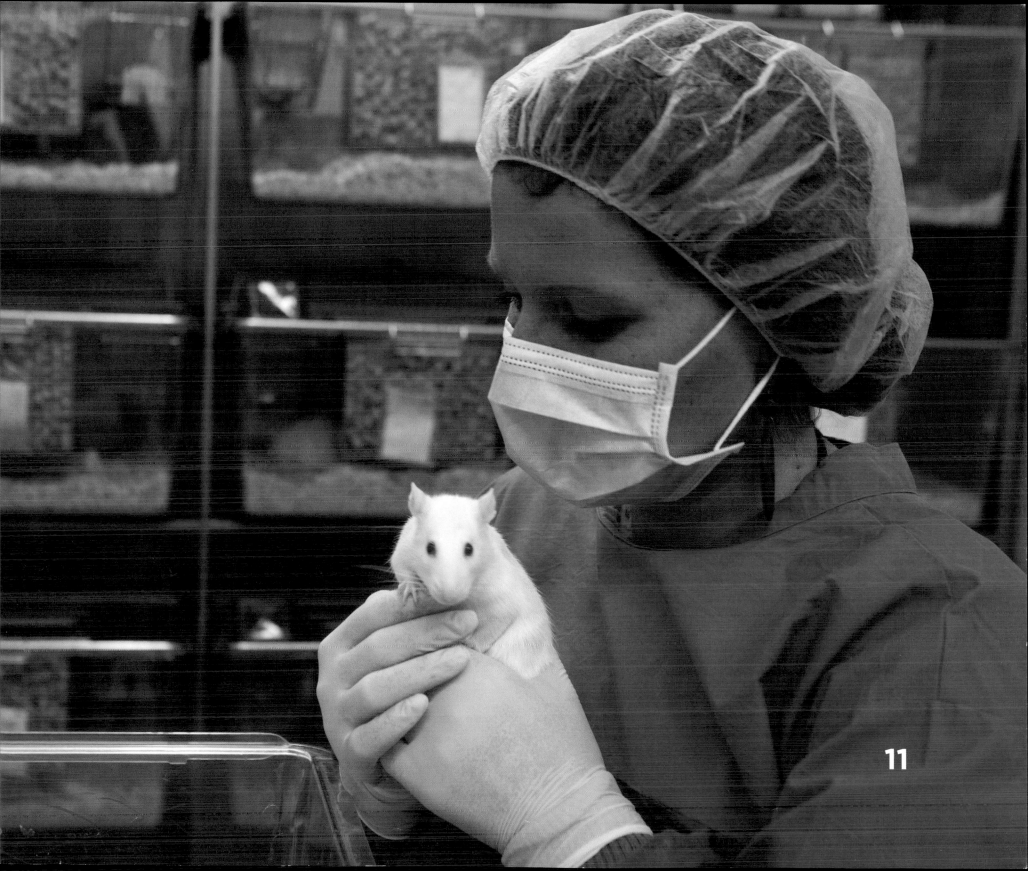

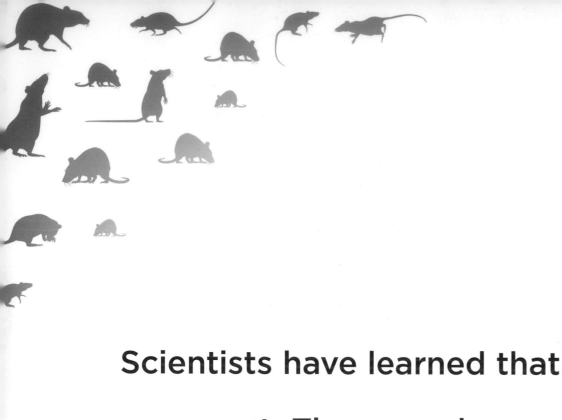

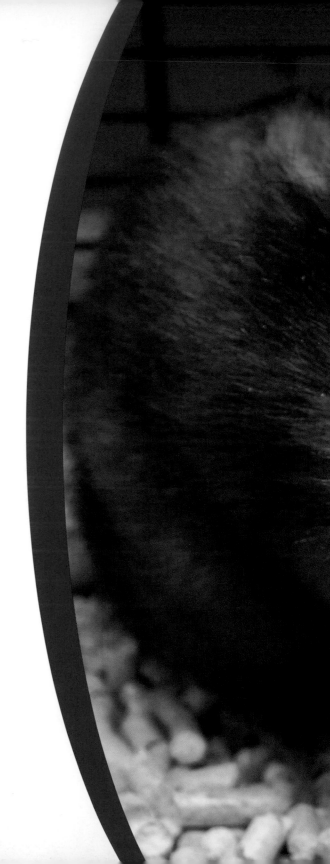

Scientists have learned that rats are smart. They are also social. They like to be with other rats.

Caring & Helpful Rodents

In one **experiment**, a rat was put in a cage. The rat could not escape the cage.

Scientists placed a piece
of chocolate inside another
cage. Rats love chocolate!

Another rat was placed outside the cages. He was free to move about. He could see that his friend was trapped. He pushed a door open to free his friend.

Then the rats freed the
chocolate. They both enjoyed
the treat. Even rats can share!

More Facts

- Rats let out a noise when they are happy. It is similar to laughter.

- Rats are very good climbers.

- Rats are smart. Pet rats can learn their names. They can even be taught to do tricks.

22

Glossary

balance – to keep upright and steady.

experiment – a scientific test that helps people learn things.

marking - a mark or pattern of marks on an animal's fur, feathers, or skin.

rodent – a small mammal that gnaws; rats, mice, squirrels, and hamsters are all examples of rodents.

Index

abdokids.com

Use this code to log on to abdokids.com and access crafts, games, videos, and more!

Abdo Kids Code:
ARK8966